Nonsense Songs, Stories, Botany and Alphabets

By

Edward Lear

(Illustrations by Edward Lear)

First published in 1871 by J.R.Bush, London

NONSENSE SONGS, STORIES, BOTANY AND ALPHABETS

(Fully Illustrated)

Edward Lear

Foreword by Tim Wapshott

CONTENTS

FOREWORD

Edward Lear

Edward Lear had been a sickly child and that, combined with an innate ability to draw, is perhaps what fuelled his imagination so relentlessly.

If he could not live in the real world, held back by assorted bronchial and respiratory illnesses early on, he would invent his own world and inhabit it with an army of friendly, comedic creations.

When it comes to nonsense rhymes, poem, limericks and songs, Lear remains The Master, and his enchanting books remain as popular as ever with children and adults alike. No-one else comes close to the phonetic word-play found in his timeless nursery classics.

Lear was born in Holloway, north London, in May 1812. The family was huge - he was the second youngest of 21 children - but his parents had little encouragement or affection for their burgeoning brood. Edward was effectively raised by his eldest sister Ann, more than 20 years his senior. She lovingly nursed him when he was ill and soon, as he grew, would be reassuring him when he was being individual, inventive and creative. She would become his lifelong mentor and companion; his best friend.

Their father Jeremiah, a City stockbroker, fell on difficult times and it hit the family hard. When Edward was just four he left with Ann, who thereafter practically raised him single-handedly man and boy.

By the time he was a young adult, Edward Lear was already gaining a reputation as an exceptional draughtsman and illustrator. He would be especially sought-after for his detailed bird drawings, employed as an artist first by the London Zoological Society. He later spent four years working for the Earl of Derby at Knowsley Hall, near Liverpool (praised for its exceptional private menagerie).

Lear's sillier side became apparent as he doodled with nonsensical, phonetical, sometimes visual, word-play. It drove his poems, limericks and songs and inspired his inventive sketches.

His first book of collected nonsense was successfully published in 1846, when Edward Lear was approaching his mid-thirties. 'A Book of Nonsense' brimmed with joyfully daft poems, limericks and doodles.

His most famous song, 'The Owl and the Pussycat', appeared in his follow-up volume of nonsense, 'Nonsense Songs, Stories, Botany and Alphabets'. With this Lear also introduced a new word to the English language, of which he was phenomenally proud: *runcible.* The word was a firm favourite, used in various songs and poems. And perfect for the arch-absurdist of the Victorians, it had no known meaning!

Runcible is arguably best-known thanks to 'The Owl and the Pussycat', who had of course dined on mince, and slices of quince, eaten with a *runcible* spoon.

Delicious.

Tim Wapshott

London
September 2020

MR LEAR'S NONSENSE SONGS

~

THE OWL AND THE PUSSYCAT

The Owl and the Pussycat

I

The Owl and the Pussy-cat went to sea
In a beautiful pea green boat,
They took some honey, and plenty of money,
Wrapped up in a five pound note.
The Owl looked up to the stars above,
And sang to a small guitar,
'O lovely Pussy! O Pussy my love,
What a beautiful Pussy you are,
You are,
You are!
What a beautiful Pussy you are!'

II

Pussy said to the Owl, 'You elegant fowl!
    How charmingly sweet you sing!
O let us be married! too long we have tarried:
    But what shall we do for a ring?'
They sailed away, for a year and a day,
    To the land where the Bong-tree grows
And there in a wood a Piggy-wig stood
    With a ring at the end of his nose,
        His nose,
        His nose,
With a ring at the end of his nose.

And there in the wood a Piggy-wig stood...

III

'Dear pig, are you willing to sell for one shilling
　　Your ring?' Said the Piggy, 'I will.'
So they took it away, and were married next
day
　　By the Turkey who lives on the hill.
They dined on mince, and slices of quince,
　　Which they ate with a runcible spoon;
And hand in hand, on the edge of the sand,
　　They danced by the light of the moon,
　　　　The moon,
　　　　The moon,
They danced by the light of the moon.

...married next day, by the Turkey who lives on the hill.

THE DUCK AND THE KANGAROO

The Duck and the Kangaroo.

I

Said the Duck to the Kangaroo,
   'Good gracious! how you hop!
Over the fields and the water too,
   As if you never would stop!
My life is a bore in this nasty pond,
And I long to go out in the world beyond!
   I wish I could hop like you!'
   Said the duck to the Kangaroo.

II

'Please give me a ride on your back!'
    Said the Duck to the Kangaroo.
'I would sit quite still, and say nothing but "Quack,"
    The whole of the long day through!
And we'd go to the Dee, and the Jelly Bo Lee,
Over the land and over the sea;--
    Please take me a ride! O do!'
    Said the Duck to the Kangaroo.

III

Said the Kangaroo to the Duck,
    'This requires some little reflection;
Perhaps on the whole it might bring me luck,
    And there seems but one objection,
Which is, if you'll let me speak so bold,
Your feet are unpleasantly wet and cold,
    And would probably give me the roo-
    Matiz!' said the Kangaroo.

Said the Kangaroo to the Duck...

IV

Said the Duck ,'As I sate on the rocks,
    I have thought over that completely,
And I bought four pairs of worsted socks
    Which fit my web-feet neatly.
And to keep out the cold I've bought a cloak,
And every day a cigar I'll smoke,
    All to follow my own dear true
    Love of a Kangaroo!'

Balance me well, dear Duck...

V

Said the Kangaroo,'I'm ready!
   All in the moonlight pale;
But to balance me well, dear Duck, sit steady!
   And quite at the end of my tail!'
So away they went with a hop and a bound,
And they hopped the whole world three times
round;
   And who so happy, -- O who,
   As the duck and the Kangaroo?

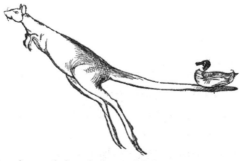

They hopped the whole world three times round.

THE DADDY LONG-LEGS AND THE FLY

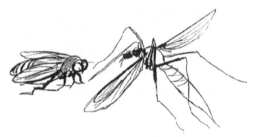

The Fly and Daddy Long-legs

I

Once Mr. Daddy Long-legs,
Dressed in brown and gray,
Walked about upon the sands
Upon a sumer's day;
And there among the pebbles,
When the wind was rather cold,
He met with Mr. Floppy Fly,
All dressed in blue and gold.
And as it was too soon to dine,
They drank some Periwinkle-wine,
And played an hour or two, or more,
At battlecock and shuttledore.

II

Said Mr. Daddy Long-legs
To Mr. Floppy Fly,
'Why do you never come to court?
I wish you'd tell me why.
All gold and shine, in dress so fine,
You'd quite delight the court.
Why do you never go at all?
I really think you ought!
And if you went, you'd see such sights!
Such rugs! Such jugs! and candle-lights!
And more than all, the King and Queen,
One in red, and one in green!'

III

'O Mr. Daddy Long-legs,'
Said Mr. Floppy Fly,
'It's true I never go to court,
And I will tell you why.
If I had six long legs like yours,
At once I'd go to court!
But oh! I can't, because my legs
Are so extremely short.
And I'm afraid the King and Queen
(One in red, and one in green)
Would say aloud, "You are not fit,
You Fly, to come to court a bit!"'

IV

'O Mr. Daddy Long-legs,'
Said Mr. Floppy Fly,
'I wish you'd sing one little song!
One mumbian melody!
You used to sing so awful well
In former days gone by,
But now you never sing at all;
I wish you'd tell me why:
For if you would, the silvery sound
Would please the shrimps and cockles round,
And all the crabs would gladly come
To hear you sing, "Ah, hum di Hum"!'

V

Said Mr. Daddy Long-legs,
'I can never sing again!
And if you wish, I'll tell you why,
Although it gives me pain.
For years I cannot hum a bit,
Or sing the smallest song;
And this the dreadful reason is,
My legs are grown too long!
My six long legs, all here and there,
Oppress my bosom with despair;
And if I stand, or lie, or sit,
I cannot sing one little bit!'

VI

So Mr. Daddy Long-legs
And Mr. Floppy Fly
Sat down in silence by the sea,
And gazed upon the sky.
They said, 'This is a dreadful thing!
The world has all gone wrong,
Since one has legs too short by half,
The other much too long!
One never more can go to court,
Because his legs have grown too short;
The other cannot sing a song,
Because his legs have grown too long!'

They found a little boat...

VII

Then Mr. Daddy Long-legs
And Mr. Floppy Fly
Rushed downward to the foamy sea
With one sponge-taneous cry;
And there they found a little boat,
Whose sails were pink and gray;
And off they sailed among the waves,
Far, and far away.
They sailed across the silent main,
And reached the great Gromboolian plain;
And there they play for evermore
At battlecock and shuttledoor.

THE JUMBLIES

The Jumblies.

I

They went to sea in a Sieve, they did,
  In a Sieve they went to sea:
In spite of all their friends could say,
On a winter's morn, on a stormy day,
  In a Sieve they went to sea!
And when the Sieve turned round and round,
And every one cried, 'You'll all be drowned!'
They called aloud, 'Our Sieve ain't big,
But we don't care a button! we don't care a fig!

In a Sieve we'll go to sea!'
    Far and few, far and few,
        Are the lands where the Jumblies live;
Their heads are green, and their hands are
blue,
        And they went to sea in a Sieve.

II

They sailed away in a Sieve, they did,
In a Sieve they sailed so fast,
  With only a beautiful pea-green veil
Tied with a riband by way of a sail,
  To a small tobacco-pipe mast;
And every one said, who saw them go,
'O won't they be soon upset, you know!
For the sky is dark, and the voyage is long,
And happen what may, it's extremely wrong
  In a Sieve to sail so fast!'
    Far and few, far and few,
        Are the lands where the Jumblies live;
Their heads are green, and their hands are
blue,
        And they went to sea in a Sieve.

III

The water it soon came in, it did,
  The water it soon came in;

So to keep them dry, they wrapped their feet
In a pinky paper all folded neat,
  And they fastened it down with a pin.
And they passed the night in a crockery-jar,
And each of them said, 'How wise we are!
Though the sky be dark, and the voyage be
long,
Yet we never can think we were rash or wrong,
  While round in our Sieve we spin!'
      Far and few, far and few,
          Are the lands where the Jumblies live;
Their heads are green, and their hands are
blue,
          And they went to sea in a Sieve.

IV

And all night long they sailed away;
  And when the sun went down,
They whistled and warbled a moony song
To the echoing sound of a coppery gong,
  In the shade of the mountains brown.
'O Timballo! How happy we are,
When we live in a Sieve and a crockery-jar,
And all night long in the moonlight pale,
We sail away with a pea-green sail,
  In the shade of the mountains brown!'
      Far and few, far and few,

    Are the lands where the Jumblies live;
Their heads are green, and their hands are
blue,
    And they went to sea in a Sieve.

                    V

They sailed to the Western Sea, they did,
  To a land all covered with trees,
And they bought an Owl, and a useful Cart,
And a pound of Rice, and a Cranberry Tart,
  And a hive of silvery Bees.
And they bought a Pig, and some green Jack-
daws,
And a lovely Monkey with lollipop paws,
And forty bottles of Ring-Bo-Ree,
  And no end of Stilton Cheese.
    Far and few, far and few,
        Are the lands where the Jumblies live;
Their heads are green, and their hands are
blue,
        And they went to sea in a Sieve.

In twenty years, they all came back...

VI

And in twenty years they all came back,
  In twenty years or more,
And every one said, 'How tall they've grown!
For they've been to the Lakes, and the Torrible
Zone,
  And the hills of the Chankly Bore!'
And they drank their health, and gave them a
feast
Of dumplings made of beautiful yeast;
And every one said, 'If we only live,
We too will go to sea in a Sieve, - - -
  To the hills of the Chankly Bore!'
      Far and few, far and few,
          Are the lands where the Jumblies live;
        Their heads are green, and their hands are
blue,
          And they went to sea in a Sieve.

THE NUTCRACKERS AND THE SUGAR-TONGS

We could ride without being instructed...

I

The Nutcrackers sate by a plate on the table,
  The Sugar-tongs sate by a plate at his side;
And the Nutcrackers said, 'Don't you wish we were able

  'Along the blue hills and green meadows to ride?
'Must we drag on this stupid existence for ever,
  'So idle so weary, so full of remorse,--
'While every one else takes his pleasure, and never
  'Seems happy unless he is riding a horse?

II

'Don't you think we could ride without being instructed?
  'Without any saddle, or bridle, or spur?
'Our legs are so long, and so aptly constructed,
  'I'm sure that an accident could not occur.
'Let us all of a sudden hop down from the table,
    'And hustle downstairs, and each jump on a horse!
'Shall we try? Shall we go! Do you think we are able?'
  The Sugar-tongs answered distinctly,'Of course!'

III

So down the long staircase they hopped in a minute,
  The Sugar-tongs snapped, and the Crackers said 'crack!'
The stable was open, the horses were in it;
  Each took out a pony, and jumped on his back.
The Cat in a fright scrambled out of the doorway,
  The Mice tumbled out of a bundle of hay,
The brown and white Rats, and the black ones from Norway,
  Screamed out, 'They are taking the horses away!'

IV

The whole of the household was filled with
amazement,
    The Cups and the Saucers danced madly about,
The Plates and the Dishes looked out of the
casement,
    The Saltcellar stood on his head with a shout,
The Spoons with a clatter looked out of the lattice,
    The Mustard-pot climbed up the Gooseberry Pies,
The Soup-ladle peeped through a heap of Veal
Patties,
        And squeaked with a ladle-like scream of
surprise.

V

The Frying-pan said, 'It's an awful delusion!'
    The Tea-kettle hissed and grew black in the face;
And they all rushed downstairs in the wildest
confusion,
    To see the great Nutcracker-Sugar-tong race.
And out of the stable, with screamings and
laughter,
        (Their ponies were cream-coloured, speckled
with brown,)
The Nutcrackers first, and the Sugar-tongs after,
    Rode all round the yard, and then all round the
town.

VI

They rode through the street, and they rode by the
station,
   They galloped away to the beautiful shore;
In silence they rode, and 'made no observation',
   Save this: 'We will never go back any more!'
And still you might hear, till they rode out of
hearing,
      The Sugar-tongs snap, and the Crackers say
'crack!'
Till far in the distance their forms disappearing,
   They faded away. -- And they never came back!

CALICO PIE

I

Calico Pie,
 The little Birds fly
Down to the calico tree,
 Their wings were blue,
 And they sang 'Tilly-loo!'
 Till away they flew,--
   And they never came back to me!
    They never came back!
    They never came back!
   They never came back to me!

Their wings were blue, and they sang 'Tilly-loo'.

II

Calico Jam,
  The little Fish swam,
Over the syllabub sea,
    He took off his hat,
  To the Sole and the Sprat,
  And the Willeby-Wat,--
But he never came back to me!
  He never came back!
  He never came back!
He never came back to me!

He took off his hat, to the Sole and the Sprat...

III

Calico Ban,
The little Mice ran,
To be ready in time for tea,
Flippity flup,
They drank it all up,
And danced in the cup,--
But they never came back to me!
They never came back!
They never came back!
They never came back to me!

They drank it all up, And danced in the cup...

IV

Calico Drum,
The Grasshoppers come,
The Butterfly, Beetle, and Bee,
Over the ground,
Around and around,
With a hop and a bound,--
But they never came back to me!

They never came back!
They never came back!
They never came back to me!

MR. AND MRS. SPIKKY SPARROW

Mr. and Mrs. Spikky Sparrow

I

On a little piece of wood,
Mr. Spikky Sparrow stood;
Mrs. Sparrow sate close by,
A-making of an insect pie,
For her little children five,
In the nest and all alive,
Singing with a cheerful smile
To amuse them all the while,
  Twikky wikky wikky wee,
  Wikky bikky twikky tee,
    Spikky bikky bee!

II

Mrs. Spikky Sparrow said,
'Spikky, Darling! in my head
'Many thoughts of trouble come,
'Like to flies upon a plum!
'All last night, among the trees,
'I heard you cough, I heard you sneeze;
'And, thought I, it's come to that
'Because he does not wear a hat!
　'Chippy wippy sikky tee!
　'Bikky wikky tikky mee!
　　'Spikky chippy wee!

III

'Not that you are growing old,
'But the nights are growing cold.
'No one stays out all night long
'Without a hat: I'm sure it's wrong!'
Mr. Spikky said 'How kind,
'Dear! you are, to speak your mind!
'All your life I wish you luck!
'You are! you are! a lovely duck!
　'Witchy witchy witchy wee!
　'Twitchy witchy witchy bee!
　　Tikky tikky tee!

IV

'I was also sad, and thinking,
'When one day I saw you winking,
'And I heard you sniffle-snuffle,
'And I saw your feathers ruffle;
'To myself I sadly said,
'She's neuralgia in her head!
'That dear head has nothing on it!
'Ought she not to wear a bonnet?
  'Witchy kitchy kitchy wee?
  'Spikky wikky mikky bee?
    'Chippy wippy chee?

V

'Let us both fly up to town!
'There I'll buy you such a gown!
'Which, completely in the fashion,
'You shall tie a sky-blue sash on.
'And a pair of slippers neat,
'To fit your darling little feet,
'So that you will look and feel,
'Quite galloobious and genteel!
  'Jikky wikky bikky see,
  'Chicky bikky wikky bee,
    'Twikky witchy wee!'

VI

So they both to London went,
Alighting on the Monument,
Whence they flew down swiftly -- pop,
Into Moses' wholesale shop;
There they bought a hat and bonnet,
And a gown with spots upon it,
A satin sash of Cloxam blue,
And a pair of slippers too.
  Zikky wikky mikky bee,
   Witchy witchy mitchy kee,
    Sikky tikky wee.

They bought a hat and a bonnet...

VII

Then when so completely drest,
Back they flew and reached their nest.
Their children cried, 'O Ma and Pa!
'How truly beautiful you are!'
Said they, 'We trust that cold or pain
'We shall never feel again!
'While, perched on tree, or house, or steeple,
'We now shall look like other people.
  'Witchy witchy witchy wee,
   'Twikky mikky bikky bee,
     Zikky sikky tee.'

THE BROOM, THE SHOVEL, THE POKER AND THE TONGS

They all took a drive in the Park...

I

The Broom and the Shovel, the Poker and the Tongs,
    They all took a drive in the Park,
And they each sang a song, Ding-a-dong, Ding-a-dong,
    Before they went back in the dark.
Mr. Poker he sate quite upright in the coach,
    Mr. Tongs made a clatter and clash,
Miss Shovel was all dressed in black (with a brooch),
    Mrs. Broom was in blue (with a sash).
      Ding-a-dong! Ding-a-dong!
      And they all sang a song!

II

'O Shovel so lovely!' the Poker he sang,
  'You have perfectly conquered my heart!
'Ding-a-dong! Ding-a-dong! If you're pleased
with my song,
  'I will feed you with cold apple tart!
'When you scrape up the coals with a delicate
sound,
  'You encapture my life with delight!
'Your nose is so shiny! your head is so round!
  'And your shape is so slender and bright!
      'Ding-a-dong! Ding-a-dong!
      'Ain't you pleased with my song?'

III

'Alas! Mrs. Broom!' sighed the Tongs in his song,
  'O is it because I'm so thin,
'And my legs are so long -- Ding-a-dong! Ding-a-
dong!
  'That you don't care about me a pin?
'Ah! fairest of creatures, when sweeping the
room,
  'Ah! why don't you heed my complaint!
'Must you needs be so cruel, you beautiful

Broom,
  'Because you are covered with paint?
    'Ding-a-dong! Ding-a-dong!
    'You are certainly wrong!'

They put on a kettle and little by little, They all became happy again.

IV

Mrs. Broom and Miss Shovel together they sang,
  'What nonsense you're singing to-day!'
Said the Shovel, 'I'll certainly hit you a bang!'
  Said the Broom, 'And I'll sweep you away!'

So the Coachman drove homeward as fast as he
could,
    Perceiving their anger with pain;
But they put on the kettle and little by little,
    They all became happy again.
      Ding-a-dong! Ding-a-dong!
      There's an end of my song!

THE TABLE AND THE CHAIR

If we took a little walk, we might have a little talk!

I

Said the Table to the Chair,
'You can hardly be aware,
'How I suffer from the heat,
'And from chilblains on my feet!
'If we took a little walk,
'We might have a little talk!
'Pray let us take the air!
'Said the Table to the Chair.

II

Said the Chair to the table,
'Now you know we are not able!
'How foolishly you talk,
'When you know we cannot walk!
'Said the Table with a sigh,
'It can do no harm to try,
'I've as many legs as you,
'Why can't we walk on two?'

III

So they both went slowly down,
And walked about the town
With a cheerful bumpy sound,
As they toddled round and round.
And everybody cried,
As they hastened to the side,
'See! the Table and the Chair
'Have come out to take the air!'

They completely lost their way...

IV

But in going down an alley,
To a castle in a valley,
They completely lost their way,
And wandered all the day,
Till, to see them safetly back,
They paid a Ducky-quack,
And a Beetle, and a Mouse,
Who took them to their house.

V

Then they whispered to each other,
'O delightful little brother!
'What a lovely walk we've taken!
'Let us dine on Beans and Bacon!
'So the Ducky and the leetle
Browny-Mousy and the Beetle
Dined and danced upon their heads
Till they toddled to their beds.

Danced upon their heads till they toddled to their beds...

MR LEAR'S NONSENSE STORIES

~

The Story of the Four Little Children
Who Went Round the World.

The History of the Seven Families
of the Lake Pipple-popple

(Chapters I-XIV)

THE STORY OF THE FOUR LITTLE CHILDREN WHO WENT ROUND THE WORLD

Violet   *Slingsby*   *Guy*   *Lionel*

Once upon a time, a long while ago, there were four little people whose names were Violet, Slingsby, Guy and Lionel and they all thought they should like to see the world. So they bought a large boat to sail quite round the world by sea, and then they were to come back on the other side by land. The boat was painted blue with green spots, and the sail was yellow with red stripes; and when they set off, they only took a small Cat to steer and look after the boat, besides an elderly Quangle-Wangle, who had to cook dinner and make the tea; for which purposes they took a large kettle.

They only took a small Cat to steer...

For the first ten days they sailed on beautifully, and found plenty to eat, as there were lots of fish, and they only had to take them out of the sea with a long spoon, when the Quangle-Wangle instantly cooked them, and the Pussy-cat was fed with the bones, with which she expressed herself pleased on the whole, so that all the party were very happy.

All the party were very happy...

During the daytime, Violet chiefly occupied herself in putting salt-water into the churn, while her three brothers churned it violently, in the hope that it would turn into butter, which it seldom, if ever did; and in the evening they all retired into the Tea-kettle, where they all managed to sleep very comfortably, while Pussy and the Quangle-Wangle managed the boat.

In the evening they all retired into the Tea-kettle...

After a time they saw some land at a distance; and when they came to it, they found it was an island made of water quite surrounded by earth. Besides that, it was bordered by evanescent isthmusses with a great Gulf-stream running about all over it, so that it was perfectly beautiful, and contained only a single tree, 503 feet high.

A single tree, 503 feet high...

When they had landed, they walked about, but found to their great surprise, that the island was quite full of veal-cutlets and chocolate-drops, and nothing else. So they all climbed up the single high tree to discover, if possible, if there were any people; but having remained on the top of the tree for a week, and not seeing anybody, they naturally concluded that there were no inhabitants, and accordingly when they came down, they loaded the boat with two thousand veal-cutlets and a million of chocolate drops, and these afforded them sustenance for more than a month, during which time they pursued their voyage with the utmost delight and apathy.

After this they came to a shore where there were no less than sixty-five great red parrots with blue tails, sitting on a rail all of a row, and all fast asleep. And I am sorry to say that the Pussy-cat and the Quangle-Wangle crept softly and bit off the tail-feathers of all the sixty-five parrots, for which Violet reproved them both severely.

Sixty-five great read parrots with blue tails...

Notwithstanding which, she proceeded to insert all the feathers, two hundred and sixty in number, in her bonnet, thereby causing it to have a lovely and glittering appearance, highly prepossessing and efficacious.

Highly prepossessing and efficacious...

The next thing that happened to them was in a narrow part of the sea, which was so entirely full of fishes that the boat could go no further; so they remained there about six weeks, till they had eaten nearly all the fishes, which were Soles, and all ready-cooked and covered with shrimp sauce, so that there was no trouble whatever. And as the few fishes that remained uneaten compleined of the cold, as well as of the difficulty they had in getting any sleep on account of the extreme noise made by the Arctic Bears and the Tropical Turnspits which frequented the neighbourhood in great numbers, Violet most amiably knitted a small woollen frock for several of the fishes, and Slingsby administered some opium drops to them, through which kindness they became quite warm and slept soundly.

A small woollen frock for several of the fishes...

Then they came to a country which was wholly covered with immense Orange-trees of a vast size, and quite full of fruit. So they all landed, taking with them a Tea-kettle, intending to gather some of the Oranges and place them in it. But while they were busy about this, a most dreadfully high wind rose, and blew out most of the Parrot-tail feathers from Violet's bonnet. That, however, was nothing compared with the calamity of the Oranges falling down on their heads by millions and millions, which thumped and bumped and bumped and thumped them all so seriously that they were obliged to run as hard as they could for their lives, besides that the sound of the Oranges rattling on the Tea-kettle was of the most fearful and amazing nature.

They all landed, taking with them a Tea-kettle...

Nevertheless they got safely to the boat, although considerably vexed and hurt; and the Quangle-Wangle's right foot was so knocked about, that he had to sit with his head in his slipper for at least a week.

He had to sit with his head in his slipper for at least a week...

This event made them all for a time rather melancholy, and perhaps they might never have become less so, had not Lionel with a most praiseworthy devotion and perseverance, continued to stand on one leg and whistle to them in a loud and lively manner, which diverted the whole party so extremely, that they gradually recovered their spirits, and agreed that whenever they should reach home they would subscribe towards a testimonial to Lionel, entirely made of Gingerbread and Raspberries, as an earnest token of their sincere and grateful infection.

Lionel

After sailing on calmly for several more days, they came to another country, where they were much pleased and surprised to see a countless multitude of white Mice with red eyes, all sitting in a great circle, slowly eating Custard Pudding with the most satisfactory and polite demeanour.

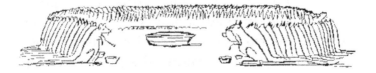

A countless multitude of white Mice.

And as the four Travellers were rather hungry, being tired of eating nothing but Soles and Oranges for so long a period, they held a council as to the propriety of asking the Mice for some of their Pudding in a humble and affecting manner, by which they could hardly be otherwise than gratified. It was agreed therefore that Guy should go and ask the Mice, which he immediately did; and the result was that they gave a Walnut-shell only half full of Custard diluted with water. Now, this displeased Guy, who said, 'Out of such a lot of Pudding as you have got, I must say you might have spared a somewhat larger quantity!' But no sooner had he finished speaking than all the Mice turned round at once, and sneezed at him in an appalling and vindictive manner, (and it is impossible to imagine a more scroobious and unpleasant sound than that caused by the simultaneous sneezing of many millions of angry Mice,) so that Guy rushed back to othe boat, having first shied his cap into into the middle of the Custard Pudding, by which means he completely spoiled the Mice's dinner.

Shied his cap into into the middle of the Custard Pudding...

By-and-by the Four Children came to a country where there were no houses, but only an incredibly innumerable number of large bottles without corks, and of a dazzling and sweetly susceptible blue colour. Each of these blue bottles contained a Blue-Bottle Fly, and all of these interesting animals live continually together in the most copious and rural harmony, nor perhaps in many parts of the world is such perfect and abject happiness to be found. Violet, and Slingsby, and Guy, and Lionel, were greatly struck with this singular and instructive settlement, and having previously asked permission of the Blue-Bottle-Flies (which was most courteously granted), the Boat was drawn up to the shore and they proceeded to make tea in front of the Bottles; but as they had no tea-leaves, they merely placed some pebbles in the hot water, and the Quangle-Wangle played some tunes over it on an Accordion, by which of course tea was made directly, and of the very best quality.

Tea was made directly, and of the very best quality.

The Four Children then entered into conversation with the Blue Bottle-Flies, who discoursed in a placid and genteel manner, though with a slightly buzzing accent, chiefly owing to the fact that they each held a small clothes-brush between their teeth which naturally occasioned a fizzy extraneous utterance.

'Why,' said Violet, 'would you kindly inform us, do you reside in hottles? and if in bottles at all, why not rather in green or purple, or indeed in yellow bottles?'

To which questions a very aged Blue-Bottle-Fly answered, 'We found the bottles here all ready to live in, that is to say, our great-great-great-great-great-grandfathers did, so we occupied them at once. And when the winter comes on, we turn the bottles upside down, and consequently rarely feel the cold at all, and you know very well that this could not be the case with bottles of any other colour than blue.'

'Of course it could not;' said Slingsby, 'but if we may take the liberty of inquiring, on what do you chiefly subsist?'

'Mainly on Oyster-patties,' said the Blue-Bottle-Fly, 'and, when these are scarce, on Raspberry vinegar and Russian leather boiled down to a jelly.'

'How delicious!' said Guy.

To which Lionel added, 'Huzz!' and all the Blue-Bottle-Flies said 'Buzz!'

At this time, an elderly Fly said it was the hour of the Evening-song to be sung; and on a signal being given all the Blue-Bottle-Flies began to buzz at once in a sumptuous and sonorous manner, the melodious and mucilaginous sounds echoing all over the waters, and resounding across the tumultuous tops of the transitory Titmice upon the intervening and verdant mountains, with a serene and sickly suavity only known to the truly virtuous. The Moon was shining slobaciously from the star-bespringled sky, while her light irrigated the smooth and shiny sides and wings and backs of the Blue-Bottle-Flies with a peculiar and trivial splendour, while all nature cheerfully responded to the cerulean and conspicuous circumstances.

In many long-after years, the four little Travellers looked back to that evening as one of the happiest in all their lives, and it was already past midnight, when - the Sail of the Boat having been set up by the Quangle-Wangle, the Tea-kettle and Churn placed in their respective positions, and the Pussy-cat stationed at the Helm - the Children each took a last and affectionate farewell of the Blue-Bottle-Flies, who walked down in a body to the water's edge to see the Travellers embark.

As a token of parting respect and esteem, Violet made a curtsey quite down to the ground, and stuck one of her few remaining Parrot-tail feathers into the back hair of the most pleasing of the Blue-Bottle-Flies, while Slingsby, Guy, and Lionel offered them three small boxes, containing respectively, Black Pins, Dried Figs, and Epsom Salts: and thus they left that happy shore for ever.

...Black Pins, Dried Figs, and Epsom Salts.

Overcome by their feelings, the Four little Travellers instantly jumped into the Tea-kettle, and fell fast asleep. But all along the shore for many hours there was distinctly heard a sound of severely suppressed sobs, and of a vague multitude of living creatures using their pocket-handkerchiefs in a subdued simultaneous snuffle - lingering sadly along the wallopping waves as the boat sailed farther and farther away from the Land of the Happy Blue-Bottle-Flies.

Nothing particular occurred for some days after these events, except that as the Travellers were passing a low tract of sand, they perceived an unusual and gratifying spectacle, namely, a large number of crabs and crawfish - perhaps six or seven hundred - sitting by the water-side, and endeavouring to disentangle a vast heap of pale pink worsted, which they moistened at intervals with a fluid composed of Lavender-water and White-wine Negus.

'Can we be of any service to you, O crusty Crabbies?' said the Four Children.

'Thank you kindly,' said the Crabs, consecutively. 'We are trying to make some worsted Mittens, but do not know how.'

On which Violet, who was perfectly acquainted with the art of mitten-making, said to the Crabs, 'Do your claws unscrew, or are they fixtures?'

'They are all made to unscrew,' said the Crabs, and forthwith they deposited a great pile of claws close to the boat, with which Violet uncombed all the pale pink worsted, and then made the loveliest Mittens with it you can imagine. These the Crabs, having resumed and screwed on their claws, placed cheerfully upon their wrists, and walked away rapidly on their hind-legs, warbling songs with a silvery voice and in a minor key.

After this the four little people sailed on again till they came to a vast and wide plain of astonishing dimensions, on which nothing whatever could be discovered at first; but as the Travellers walked onward, there appeared in the extreme and dim distance a single object, which on a nearer approach and on an accurately cutaneous inspection, seemed to be somebody in a large white wig sitting on an arm-chair made of Sponge Cakes and Oyster-shells. 'It does not quite look like a human being,' said Violet, doubtfully; nor could they make out what it really was, till the Quangle-Wangle (who had previously been round the world), exclaimed softly in a loud voice, 'It is the Co-operative Cauliflower!'

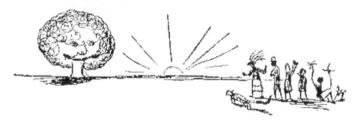

The Co-operative Cauliflower.

And so in truth it was, and they soon found that what they had taken for an immense wig was in reality the top of the cauliflower, and that he had no feet at all, being able to walk tolerably well with a fluctuating and graceful movement on a single cabbage stalk, an accomplishment which naturally saved him the expense of stock ings and shoes.

Presently, while the whole party from the boat was gazing at him with mingled affection and disgust, he suddenly arose, and in a somewhat plumdomphious manner hurried off towards the setting sun, - his steps supported by two superincumbent confidential cucumbers, and a large number of Waterwagtails proceeding in advance of him by three-and-three in a row - till he finally disappeared on the brink of the western sky in a crystal cloud of sudorific sand.

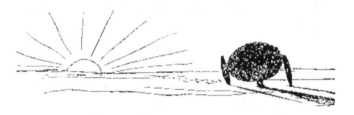

In a somewhat plumdomphious manner
hurried off towards the setting sun...

So remarkable a sight of course impressed the Four Children very deeply; and they returned immediately to their boat with a strong sense of undeveloped asthma and a great appetite.

Shortly after this the Travellers were obliged to sail directly below some high overhanging rocks, from the top of one of which, a particularly odious little boy, dressed in rose-coloured knickerbockers, and with a pewter plate upon his head, threw an enormous Pumpkin at the boat, by which it was instantly upset.

*A particularly odious little boy, dressed in
rose-coloured knickerbockers...*

But this upsetting was of no consequence, because all the party knew how to swim very well, and in fact they preferred swimming about till after the moon rose, when the water growing chilly, they sponge-taneously entered the boat. Meanwhile the Quangle-Wangle threw back the Pumpkin with immense force, so that it hit the rocks where the malicious little boy in rose-coloured knickerbockers was sitting, when, being quite full of Lucifer-matches, the Pumpkin exploded surreptitiously into a thousand bits, whereupon the rocks instantly took fire, and the odious little boy became unpleasantly hotter and hotter and hotter, till his knickerbockers were turned quite green, and his nose was burned off.

Two or three days after this had happened, they came to another place, where they found nothing at all except some wide and deep pits full of Mulberry Jam. This is the property of the tiny Yellow-nosed Apes who abound in these districts, and who store up the Mulberry Jam for their food in winter, when they mix it with pellucid pale periwinkle soup, and serve it out in Wedgwood China bowls, which grow freely over that part of the country. Only one of the Yellow-nosed Apes was on the spot, and he was fast asleep: yet the Four Travellers and the Quangle-Wangle and Pussy were so terrified by the violence and sanguinary sound of his snoring, that they merely took a small cupful of the Jam, and returned to re-embark in their Boat without delay.

What was their horror on seeing the boat (including the Churn and the Tea-kettle), in the mouth of an enormous Seeze Pyder, an aquatic and ferocious creature truly dreadful to behold, and happily only met with in those excessive longitudes. In a moment the beautiful boat was bitten into fifty-five-thousand-million-hundred-billion bits, and it instantly became quite clear that Violet, Slingsby, Guy, and Lionel could no longer preliminate their voyage by sea.

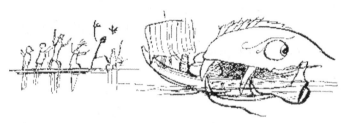

An enormous Seeze Pyder, an aquatic and ferocious creature...

The Four Travellers were therefore obliged to resolve on pursuing their wanderings by land, and very fortunately there happened to pass by at that moment, an elderly Rhinoceros, on which they seized; and all four mounting on his back, the Quangle-Wangle sitting on his horn and holding on by his ears, and the Pussy-cat swinging at the end of his tail, they set off, having only four small beans and three pounds of mashed potatoes to last through their whole journey.

They were, however, able to catch numbers of the chickens and turkeys, and other birds who incessantly alighted on the head of the Rhinoceros for the purpose of gathering the seeds of the rhododendron plants which grew there, and these creatures they cooked in the most translucent and satisfactory manner, by means of a fire lighted on the end of the Rhinoceros' back. A crowd of Kangaroos and Gigantic Cranes accompanied them, from feelings of curiosity and complacency, so that they were never at a loss for company, and went onward as it were in a sort of profuse and triumphant procession.

A crowd of Kangaroos and Gigantic Cranes accompanied them...

Thus, in less than eighteen weeks, they all arrived safely at home, where they were received by their admiring relatives with joy tempered with contempt; and where they finally resolved to carry out the rest of their travelling plans at some more favourable opportunity.

As for the Rhinoceros, in token of their grateful adherence, they had him killed and stuffed directly, and then set him up outside the door of their father's house as a Diaphanous Doorscraper.

A Diaphanous Doorscraper.

THE HISTORY OF THE
SEVEN FAMILIES OF THE
LAKE PIPPLE-POPPLE

~

CHAPTER I
INTRODUCTORY

In former days -- that is to say, once upon a time, there lived in the Land of Gramblamble, Seven Families. They lived by the side of the great Lake Pipple-popple (one of the Seven Families, indeed, lived in the Lake), and on the outskirts of the City of Tosh, which, excepting when it was quite dark, they could see plainly. The names of all these places you have probably heard of, and you have only not to look in your Geography books to find out all about them.

Now the Seven Families who lived on the borders of the great Lake Pipple-popple, were as follows in the next Chapter.

CHAPTER II
THE SEVEN FAMILIES

There was a Family of Two old Parrots and Seven young Parrots.

Nine Parrots.

There was a Family of Two old Storks and Seven young Storks.

Nine Storks.

There was a Family of Two old Geese, and Seven young Geese.

Nine Geese.

There was a Family of Two old Owls, and Seven young Owls.

Nine Owls.

There was a Family of Two Old Guinea Pigs and
Seven young Guinea Pigs.

Nine Guinea Pigs.

There was a Family of Two old Cats and Seven
young Cats.

Nine Cats.

And there was a Family of Two old Fishes and Seven young Fishes.

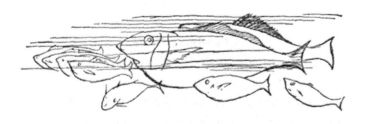

Nine Fishes.

CHAPTER III
THE HABITS OF THE SEVEN FAMILIES

The Parrots lived upon the Soffsky-Poffsky trees, -- which were beautiful to behold, and covered with blue leaves, -- and they fed upon fruit, artichokes, and striped beetles.

The Storks walked in and out of the Lake Pipple-popple, and ate frogs for breakfast and buttered toast for tea, but on account of the extreme length of their legs, they could not sit down, and so they walked about continually.

The Geese, having webs to their feet, caught quantities of flies, which they ate for dinner.

The Owls anxiously looked after mice, which they caught and made into sago puddings.

The Guinea Pigs toddled about the gardens, and ate lettuces and Cheshire cheese.

The Cats sate still in the sunshine, and fed upon sponge biscuits.

The Fishes lived in the Lake, and fed chiefly on boiled periwinkles.

And all these Seven Families lived together in the utmost fun and felicity.

CHAPTER IV
THE CHILDREN OF THE SEVEN FAMILIES ARE SENT AWAY

One day all the Seven Fathers and the Seven
Mothers of the Seven Families agreed that they
would send their children out to see the world.

So they called them all together, and gave them
each eight shillings and some good advice, some
chocolate drops, and a small green morocco
pocket-book to set down their expenses in.

They then particularly entreated them not
to quarrel, and all the parents sent off their
children with a parting injunction.

'If,' said the old Parrots, 'you find a Cherry, do not
fight about who should have it.'

'And,' said the old Storks, 'if you find a Frog,
divide it carefully into seven bits, but on no
account quarrel about it.'

And the old Geese said to the Seven young Geese,
'Whatever you do, be sure you do not touch a
Plum-pudding Flea.'

And the old Owls said, 'If you find a Mouse, tear
him up into seven slices, and eat him cheerfully,

but without quarrelling.'

And the old Guinea Pigs said, 'Have a care that you eat your Lettuces, should you find any, ot greedily but calmly.'

And the old Cats said, 'Be particularly careful not to meddle with a Clangle-Wangle, if you should see one.'

And the old Fishes said, 'Above all things avoid eating a blue Boss-woss, for they do not agree with Fishes, and give them pain in their toes.'

So all the Children of each Family thanked their parents, and making in all forty-nine polite bows, they went into the wide world.

CHAPTER V
THE HISTORY OF THE SEVEN YOUNG PARROTS

The Seven young Parrots had not gone far, when they saw a tree with a single Cherry on it, which the oldest Parrot picked instantly, but the other six, being extremely hungry, tried to get it also. On which all the Seven began to fight, and they scuffled,

and huffled,
and ruffled
and shuffled,
and puffled,
and muffled
and buffled,
and duffled,
and fluffled,
and guffled,
and bruffled, and

screamed, and shrieked, and squealed, and squeaked, and clawed, and snapped, and bit, and bumped, and thumped, and dumped, and flumped each other, till they were all torn into little bits, and at last there was nothing left to record this painful incident, except the Cherry and seven small green feathers.

They scuffled, and huffled, and ruffled...

And that was the vicious and voluble end of the Seven young Parrots.

CHAPTER VI
THE HISTORY OF THE SEVEN YOUNG STORKS

When the Seven young Storks set out, they walked or flew fo fourteen weeks in a straight line, and for six weeks more in a crooked one; and after that they ran as hard as they could for one hundred and eight miles: and after that they stood still and made a himmeltanious chatter-clatter-blattery noise with their bills.

About the same time they perceived a large Frog, spotted with green, and with a sky-blue stripe under each ear.

So being hungry, they immediately flew at him, and were going to divide him into seven pieces, when they began to quarrel as to which of his legs should be taken off first. one said this, and another said that, and while they were all quarrelling the Frog hopped away. And when they saw that he was gone, they began to chatter-clatter:

> and huffled,
> blatter-platter,
> patter-blatter,
> matter-clatter,
> flatter-quatter,

more violently than ever. And after they had fought for a week they pecked each each other all to little pieces, so that at last nothing was left of any of them except their bills,

And that was the end of the Seven young Storks.

They pecked each other all to little pieces...

CHAPTER VII
THE HISTORY OF THE SEVEN YOUNG GEESE

When the Seven young Geese began to travel, they went over a large plain, on which there was but one tree, and that was a very bad one.

So four of them went up to the top of it, and looked about them, while the other three waddled up and down, and repeated poetry, and their last six lessons in Arithmetic, Geography, and Cookery.

Presently they perceived, a long way off, an object of the most interesting and obese appearance, having a perfectly round body, exactly resembling a boiled plum-pudding, with two little wings, and a beak, and three feathers growing out of his head, and only one leg.

So after a time all the Seven young Geese said to each other, 'Beyond all doubt this beast must be a Plum-pudding Flea!'

On which they uncautiously began to sing aloud,

'Plum-pudding Flea,

'Plum-pudding Flea,
'Wherever you be,
'O come to our tree,
And listen, O listen, O listen to me!'

And no sooner had they sung this verse then
the Plum-pudding Flea began to hop and skip on
his one leg with the most dreadful velocity, and
came straight to the tree, where he stopped and
looked about him in a vacant and voluminous
manner.

On which the Seven young Geese were greatly
alarmed, and all of a tremble-bemble: so one of
them put out his great neck, and just touched
him with the tip of his bill, -- but no sooner
had he done this than the Plum-pudding Flea
skipped and hopped about more and more
and higher and higher, after which he opened
his mouth, and, to the great surprise and
indignation of the Seven Geese, began to bark so
loudly and furiously and terribly that they were
totally unable to bear the noise, and by degrees
every one of them suddenly tumbled down quite
dead.

So that was the end of the Seven young Geese.

The Plum-pudding Flea began to hop and skip on his one leg...

CHAPTER VIII

THE HISTORY OF THE SEVEN YOUNG OWLS

When the Seven young Owls set out, they sate every now and then on the branches of old trees, and never went far at one time.

And one night when it was quite dark, they thought they heard a Mouse, but as the gas lights were not lighted, they could not see him.

So they called out, 'Is that a Mouse?'

On which a Mouse answered, 'Squeaky-peeky-weeky, yes it is.'

And immediately all the young Owls threw themselves off the tree, meaning to alight on the ground; but they did not perceive that there was a large well below them, into which they all fell superficially, and were every one of them drowned in less than half a minute.

There was a large well below them...

So that was the end of the Seven young Owls.

CHAPTER IX

THE HISTORY OF THE SEVEN YOUNG GUINEA PIGS

The Seven young Guinea Pigs went into a garden full of Gooseberry-bushes and Tiggory-trees, under one of which they fell asleep. When they awoke, they saw a large Lettuce which had grown out of the ground while they had been sleeping, and which had an immense number of green leaves. At which they all exclaimed:

> 'Lettuce! O Lettuce!
> 'Let us, O let us,
> 'O Lettuce leaves,
> 'O let us leave this tree and eat
> 'Lettuce, O let us, Lettuce leaves!'

And instantly the Seven young Guinea Pigs rushed with such extreme force against the Lettuce-plant, and hit their heads so vividly against its stalk, that the concussion brought on directly an incipient transitional inflammation of their noses, which grew worse and worse and worse and worse till it incidentally killed them all Seven.

And that was the end of the Seven young Guinea Pigs.

Lettuce! O Lettuce!

CHAPTER X

THE HISTORY OF THE SEVEN YOUNG CATS

The Seven young Cats set off on their travels with great delight and rapacity. But, on coming to the top of a high hill, they perceived at a long distance off a Clangle-Wangle (or, as it is more properly written, Clangel-Wangel), and in spite of the warning they had had, they ran straight up to it.

(Now the Clangle-Wangle is a most dangerous and delusive beast, and by no means commonly to be met with. They live in the water as well as on land, using their long tail as a sail when in the former element. Their speed is extreme, but their habits of life are domestic and superfluous, and their general demeanour pensive and pellucid. On summer evenings they may sometimes be observed near the Lake Pipple-popple, standing on their heads and humming their national melodies: they subsist entirely on vegetables, excepting when they eat veal, or mutton, or pork, or beef, or fish, or saltpetre.)

The moment the Clangle-Wangle saw the Seven young Cats approach, he ran away; and as he ran straight on for four months, and the Cats, though they continued to run, could never overtake him, -- they all gradually died of fatigue and of exhaustion, and never afterwards recovered.

And this was the end of the Seven young Cats.

The moment the Clangle-Wangle saw the Seven young Cats approach, he ran away...

CHAPTER XI

The Seven young Fishes swam across the Lake Pipple-popple, and into the river, and into the Ocean, where most unhappily for them, they saw on the 15th day of their travels, a bright blue Boss-Woss, and instantly swam after him. But the Blue Boss-Woss plunged into a perpendicular,

> spicular,
> > orbicular,
> > > quadrangular,
> > > > circular depth of soft

mud,

where in fact his house was.

And the Seven young Fishes, swimming with great uncomfortable velocity, plunged also into the mud quite against their will, and not being accustomed to it, were all suffocated in a very short period.

And that was the end of the Seven young Fishes.

They saw on the 15th day of their travels,
a bright blue Boss-Woss...

CHAPTER XII
OF WHAT OCCURRED SUBSEQUENTLY

After it was known that the

Seven young Parrots,
     and the Seven young Storks,
     and the Seven young Geese,
     and the Seven young Owls,
     and the Seven young Guinea Pigs,
     and the Seven young Cats,
     and the Seven young Fishes,

were all dead, then the Frog, and the Plum-pudding Flea, and the Mouse, and the Clangel Wangel, and the Blue Boss Woss, all met together to rejoice over their good fortune.

A circular arrangement at their base...

And they collected the Seven Feathers of the Seven young Parrots, and the Seven Bills of the Seven young Storks, and the Lettuce, and the other objects in a circular arrangement at their base, they danced a hornpipe round all these memorials until they were quite tired: after which they gave a tea-party, and a garden-party, and a ball, and a concert, and then returned to their respective homes full of joy and respect, sympathy, satisfaction, and disgust.

CHAPTER XIII

OF WHAT BECAME OF THE PARENTS OF
THE FORTY-NINE CHILDREN

But when the two old Parrots,
    and the two old Storks,
    and the two old Geese,
    and the two old Owls,
    and the two old Guinea Pigs,
    and the two old Cats,
    and the two old Fishes,
became aware by reading in the newspapers, of
the calamitous extinction of the whole of their
families, they refused all further sustenance;
and sending out to various shops, they
purchased great quantities of Cayenne Pepper,
and Brandy, and Vinegar, and blue Sealing-wax,
besides Seven immense glass Bottles with air-
tight stoppers. And having dome this, they ate
a light supper of brown bread and Jerusalem
Artichokes, and took an affecting and formal
leave of the whole of their acquaintance, which
was very numerous and distinguished, and
select, and responsible, and ridiculous.

CHAPTER XIV

CONCLUSION

And after this, they filled the bottles with
the ingredients for pickling, and each couple
jumped into a separate bottle, by which effort of
course they all died immediately, and become
thoroughly pickled in a few minutes; having
previously made their wills (by the assistance
of the most eminent Lawyers of the District), in
which they left strict
orders that the Stoppers of the Seven Bottles
should be carefully sealed up with the blue
Sealing-wax they had purchased; and that they
themselves in the Bottles should be presented
to the principal museum of the city of Tosh,
to be labelled with Parchment or any other
anticongenial succedaneum, and to be placed
on a marble table with silver-gilt legs, for the
daily inspection and contemplation, and for the
perpetual benefit of the pusillanimous public.

Carefully sealed up with the blue Sealing-wax...

And if ever you happen to go to Gramble-Blamble, and visit that museum in the city of Tosh, look for them on the Ninety-eighth table in the Four hundred and twenty-seventh room of the right-hand corridor of the left wing of the Central Quadrangle of that magnificent building; for if you do not, you certainly will not see them.

MR LEAR'S NONSENSE BOTANY

~

BottlePhorkia Spoonifolia

Smalltoothcombia Domesticus

BlueBottlia Buzztilentia

Pollybirdia Singularis

Plumbunnia Nurtitiosa

Manypeeplia Upsiddownia

Guittaria Pensilis

Cockatooca Superba

Baccopipia Gracillis

Fishia Marina

Pigglawiggla Pyramisdalis

BOTTLEPHORKIA
SPOONIFOLIA

SMALLTOOTHCOMBIA DOMESTICA

BLUEBOTTLIA
BUZZTILENTIA

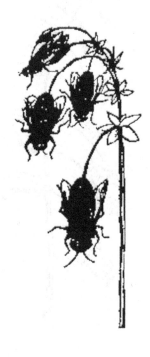

POLLYBIRDIA SINGULARIS

PHATTFACIA STUPENDA

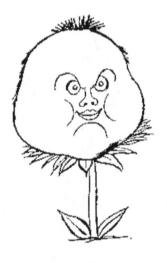

PLUMBUNNIA
NURTITIOSA

MANYPEEPLIA
UPSIDDOWNIA

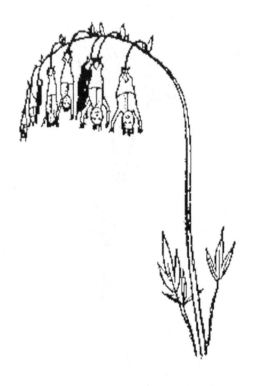

GUITTARA PENSILIS

COCKATOOCA SUPERBA

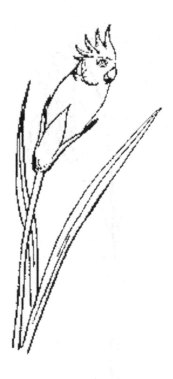

BACCOPIPIA GRACILLIS

FISHIA MARINA

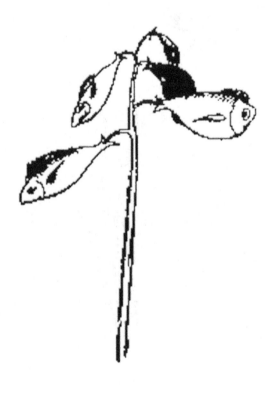

PIGGIAWIGGIA
PYRAMIDALIS

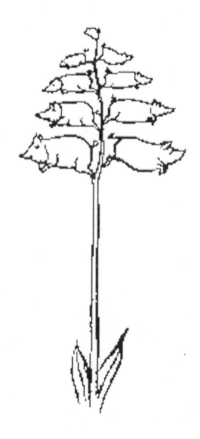

MR LEAR'S NONSENSE ALPHABETS

~

ALPHABET POEM I

A

A was an ant
Who seldom stood still,
And who made a nice house
In the side of a hill.

a

Nice little ant!

B

B was a book
With a binding of blue,
And pictures and stories
For me and for you.

b

Nice little book!

C

C was a cat
Who ran after a rat;
But his courage did fail
When she seized on his tail.

c

Crafty old cat!

D

D was a duck
With spots on his back,
Who lived in the water,
And always said "Quack!"

d

Dear little duck!

E

E was an elephant,
Stately and wise:
He had tusks and a trunk,
And two queer little eyes.

e

Oh, what funny small eyes!

F

F was a fish
Who was caught in a net;
But he got out again,
And is quite alive yet.

f

Lively young fish!

G

G was a goat
Who was spotted with brown:
When he did not lie still
He walked up and down.

g

Good little goat!

H

H was a hat
Which was all on one side;
Its crown was too high,
And its brim was too wide.

h

Oh, what a hat!

I

I was some ice
So white and so nice,
But which nobody tasted;
And so it was wasted.

i

All that good ice!

J

J was a jackdaw
Who hopped up and down
In the principal street

Of a neighboring town.

j

All through the town!

K

K was a kite
Which flew out of sight,
Above houses so high,
Quite into the sky.

k

Fly away, kite!

L

L was a light
Which burned all the night,
And lighted the gloom
Of a very dark room.

l

Useful nice light!

M

M was a mill
Which stood on a hill,
And turned round and round
With a loud hummy sound.

m

Useful old mill!

N

N was a net
Which was thrown in the sea
To catch fish for dinner
For you and for me.

n

Nice little net!

O

O was an orange
So yellow and round:
When it fell off the tree,

It fell down to the ground.

o

Down to the ground!

P

P was a pig,
Who was not very big;
But his tail was too curly,
And that made him surly.

p

Cross little pig!

Q

Q was a quail
With a very short tail;
And he fed upon corn
In the evening and morn.

q

Quaint little quail!

R

R was a rabbit,
Who had a bad habit
Of eating the flowers
In gardens and bowers.

r

Naughty fat rabbit!

S

S was the sugar-tongs,
sippity-see,
To take up the sugar
To put in our tea.

s

sippity-see!

T

T was a tortoise,
All yellow and black:
He walked slowly away,

And he never came back.

t

Torty never came back!

U

U was an urn
All polished and bright,
And full of hot water
At noon and at night.

u

Useful old urn!

V

V was a villa
Which stood on a hill,
By the side of a river,
And close to a mill.

v

Nice little villa!

W

W was a whale
With a very long tail,
Whose movements were frantic
Across the Atlantic.

w

Monstrous old whale!

X

X was King Xerxes,
Who, more than all Turks, is
Renowned for his fashion
Of fury and passion.

x

Angry old Xerxes!

Y

Y was a yew,
Which flourished and grew
By a quiet abode

Near the side of a road.

y

Dark little yew!

Z

Z was some zinc,
So shiny and bright,
Which caused you to wink
In the sun's merry light.

z

Beautiful zinc!

ALPHABET POEM II

A was once an ant,
Tiny,
Busy,
Speedy,
Shiny
In the groundy
Little ant!

A was once a little ant,
Antsy
Fantsy
Mantsy
Antsy,
Fantsy anty,
Little ant!

B was once a little bat,
Batsy,
Watsy,
Fatsy,
Batsy,
Bumpy smacky
Little bat!

C was once a little cat,

Batty,
Catty,
Fatty,
Jatty,
Fatty batty,
Little cat!

C was once a little cow,
Cowy,
Bowy,
Wowy,
Howy,
Powy cowy,
Little cow!

D was once a little dog,
Doggy,
Woggy,
Loggy,
Doggy,
Fasty-runner,
Little doggy!

E was once the whole wide earth,
Earthy,
Mearthy,
Girthy,
It gave birthy
To this new earthy,
This whole wide earth!

G was once a little goat,
Goaty,
Woaty,
Foaty,
Goaty,
Baa, baa oaty,
Little goat!

H was once a little hawk,
Hawky,
Lawky,
Stawky,
Hawky,
Smawky hawky,
Little hawk!

I was once a little iguana,
Igy,
Wigy,
Ligy,
Igy,
Silly willy,
Little iguana!

J was once a little juke box,
Boxy,
Koxy,
Loxy,
Boxy,
Wide insidy,
Little juke box!

K was once a little kit,
Kitty,
Bitty,
Itty,
Witty,
Icky kitty,
Little kit!

L was once little lion,
Mindon,
Gion,
Bion,
Sighon
Gooey zion,
Little lion!

M is an 'm' you see,
Memmy,
Temmy,
Semmy,
Shemmy,
Now 'm' is a moose you see,
But she doesn't want to be!

O was once a little ox,
Oxy,
Woxy,
Foxy,
Noxy,
Run run oxy,

Little Ox!

P was once a plump old lady,
Plumpy,
Pumpy,
Tunky,
Wunky,
Plumpy pumpy,
Little old lady!

Q was once a little quail,
Quaily,
Scaly,
Whaly,
Quaily,
Paly quaily,
Little quail!

S was once a little snake,
Snakey,
Bakey,
Kakey,
Sakey,
In a jungel,
Little snake!

T was once a little turtle,
Turtally,
Urtally,
Nurtally,
Turtally,

Murtally burtally,
Little turtle!

U was once a little unicorn,
Unicorny,
Tricorny,
Minocorny,
Unicorny,
In a barn,
Little unicorn!

V was once a little van,
Vanny,
Flanny,
Manny
Vanny,
Drive really fasty,
Little van!

W was once a little witch,
Witchy,
Twitchy,
Cwitchy,
Witc hy,
Fly real high,
Little witch!

X was once a little x-man,
Mexman,
Nexman,
Pexman,

Mexman ,
X-man has big claws,
Little x-man!

Y was once a little yarn,
Yarny,
Carny,
Larny,
Yarny,
Rolly yarny,
Little yarn!

Z was once a little zucchini,
Winey,
Tiney,
Liney,
Winey,
Tinky zinky,
Little letter z!

ALPHABET POEM III

A was once an apple pie,
Pidy
Widy
Tidy
Pidy
Nice insidy
Apple Pie!

B was once a little bear,
Beary!
Wary!
Hairy!
Beary!
Taky cary!
Little Bear!

C was once a little cake,
Caky
Baky
Maky
Caky
Taky Caky,
Little Cake!

D was once a little doll,

Dolly
Molly
Polly
Nolly
Nursy Dolly
Little Doll!

E was once a little eel,
Eely,
Weely
Peely
Eely
Twirly, Tweedy
Little Eel!

F was once a little fish,
Fishy
Wishy
Squishy
Fishy
In a Dishy
Little Fish!

G was once a little goose,
Goosy
Moosy
Boosy
Goosey
Waddly-woosy
Little Goose!

H was once a little hen,
Henny
Chenny
Tenny
Henny
Eggsy-any
Little Hen?

I was once a bottle of ink,
Inky
Dinky
Thinky
Inky
Black Minky
Bottle of Ink!

J was once a jar of jam,
Jammy
Mammy
Clammy
Jammy
Sweety-Swammy
Jar of Jam!

K was once a little kite,
Kity
Whity
Flighty
Kity
Out of sighty-
Little Kite!

L was once a little lark,
Larky!
Marky!
Harky!
Larky!
In the Parky,
Little Lark!

M was once a little mouse,
Mousey
Bousey
Sousy
Mousy
In the Housy
Little Mouse!

N was once a little needle,
Needly
Tweedly
Threedly
Needly
Wisky-wheedly
Little Needle!

O was once a little owl,
Owly
Prowly
Howly
Owly
Browny fowly

Little Owl!

P was once a little pump,
Pumpy
Slumpy
Flumpy
Pumpy
Dumpy, Thumpy
Little Pump!

Q was once a little quail,
Quaily
Faily
Daily
Quaily
Stumpy-taily
Little Quail!

R was once a little rose,
Rosy
Posy
Nosy
Rosy
Bows-y - grows-y
Little Rose!

S was once a little shrimp,
Shrimpy
Nimpy
Flimpy
Shrimpy

Jumpy-jimpy
Little Shrimp!

T was once a little thrush,
Thrushy!
Hushy!
Bushy!
Thrushy!
Flitty-Flushy
Little Thrush!

U was once a little urn,
Urny
Burny
Turny
Urny
Bubbly-burny
Little Urn!

V was once a little vine,
Viny
Winy
Twiny
Viny
Twisty-twiny
Little Vine!

W was once a whale,
Whaly
Scaly
Shaly

Whaly
Tumbly-taily
Mighty Whale!

X was once a great king Xerxes,
Xerxy
Perxy
Turxy
Xerxy
Linxy Lurxy
Great King Xerxes!

Y was once a little yew,
Yewdy
Fewdy
Crudy
Yewdy
Growdy, grewdy,
Little Yew!

Z was once a piece of zinc,
Tinky
Winky
Blinky
Tinky
Tinkly Minky
Piece of Zinc!

ALPHABET POEM IV

A tumbled down, and hurt his Arm, against a bit of wood.

B said, "My Boy, O! do not cry' it cannot do you good!"

C said, "A Cup of Coffee hot can't do you any harm."

D said, "A Doctor should be fetched, and he would cure the arm."

E said, "An Egg beat up in milk would quickly make him well."

F said, "A Fish, if broiled, might cure, if only by the smell."

G said, "Green Gooseberry fool, the best of cures I hold."

H said, "His Hat should be kept on, keep him from the cold."

I said, "Some Ice upon his head will make him

better soon."

J said, "Some Jam, if spread on bread, or given in a spoon."

K said, "A Kangaroo is here,—this picture let him see."

L said, "A Lamp pray keep alight, to make some barley tea."

M said, "A Mulberry or two might give him satisfaction."

N said, "Some Nuts, if rolled about, might be a slight attraction."

O said, "An Owl might make him laugh, if only it would wink."

P said, "Some Poetry might be read aloud, to make him think."

Q said, "A Quince I recommend, ---A Quince, or else a Quail."

R said, "Some Rats might make him move, if fastened by their tail."

S said, "A Song should now be sung, in hopes to make him laugh!"

T said, "A Turnip might avail, if sliced or cut in half."

U said, "An Urn, with water hot, place underneath his chin!"

V said, "I'll stand upon a chair, and play a Violin!"

W said, "Some Whiskey-Whizzgigs fetch, some marbles and a ball!"

X said, "Some double XX ale would be the best of all!"

Y said, "Some Yeast mised up with salt would make a perfect plaster!"

Z said, "Here is a box of Zinc! Get in my little master!
We'll shut you up! We'll nail you down!
We will, my little master!
We think we've all heard quite enough of this sad disaster!"

ABOUT THE AUTHOR

Edward Lear

May 12, 1812 - January 29, 1888

AFTERWORD

*Edward Lear was born in Holloway, north London, and became the master of Victorian nonsensical limericks, poems, stories, alphabets and drawings. '**Nonsense, Songs, Stories, Botany and Alphabets**' was first published in 1871 by J.R.Bush, Charing Cross, London in 1871.*

Edward Lear

Edward Lear was born in Holloway, north London, in 1812. In the 1800s, Holloway was part of London's suburban landscape, home to aspirational middle-class families who thrived there in Victorian times. Many, including

Lear's father Jeremiah, worked a few miles away in the City of London and doubtless commuted daily, depending on his fortunes, by black hackney carriage or a London omnibus.

Holloway became one of the capital's first proper suburbs of the middle-classes of the 1800s.

Nor did its suburban significance go unnoticed by the retailing Jones Brothers, who dominated Holloway Road for the latter part of the century with their emporium of upward mobility. The Jones Brothers' departmental store was a palace of light and wonder to all who entered.

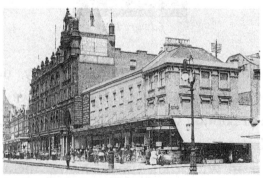

Jones Brothers Departmental Store, circa 1910

Today, Peter Jones and John Lewis, along with their grocery stablemate Waitrose, face a changing retail landscape in which they try against growing odds to still remain a relevant arbiter of British middle-class taste.

Back in the 1850s, and considerably less feted by the middle-class locals, was heinous Holloway Prison. The forbidding, soulless women-only penitentiary was home to some of London's most notorious murderers and thieves. (In time it also shamefully housed more than 20 suffragettes, including Emmiline and Christine Pankhurst.)

Emmiline and Christine Pankhurst
Holloway Prison

Towards the end of the 1800s, an embryonic Arsenal football club had arrived down the road from Holloway, formatively kicking around some early success on the pitch.

Arsenal football team, circa 1899

And as the Gunners were getting going, the general public at large - for whom funny is funny, or rather amused is amused - closed the century still savouring the uniquely lyrical stylings of Edward Lear.

Lear's books 'A Book of Nonsense' and 'Nonsense Songs, Stories, Botany and Alphabets' have rarely, if ever, been out of print since first publication.

This is a mark of their timeless appeal to

generations of families - and to legions of parents who were enraptured when Lear's nonsensical jewels were first read to them at bedtime by their folks, and who eagerly passed on such heavenly joy to their own children when the time came.

Runcible praise indeed.

Tim Wapshott

London
September 2020

DEDICATION

It seemed inappropriate to mention any dedication at the start of this book of Edward Lear's timeless gems.

It is hoped that this 2020 outing might find a few new fans, both young and old, who will delight as others before them in Lear's delicious imagination and delectable word-play.

This 2020 outing is dedicated to Elizabeth, and

Arabella
Arlo
Edison
Leo
Maisie Mae
Nellie
Oliver
Rocco

and

Winnie

...in the hope it, too, brings them boundless joy in the years ahead...

OTHER BOOKS BY TIM WAPSHOTT

Other books by Tim Wapshott include:

Mercury and Me, Jim Hutton with Tim Wapshott

Older, the Definitive Biography of George Michael, Nicholas and Tim Wapshott

The Diary of a Nobody, George Grossmith (Foreword)

Nonsense Songs, Stories, Botany and Alphabets, Edward Lear (Foreword)

Just So Stories for Little Children, Rudyard Kipling (Foreword)

Made in United States
North Haven, CT
04 December 2024

61557401R00095